The Fairly Scary Fairy

'The Fairly Scary Fairy'
An original concept by Kate Poels
© Kate Poels 2023

Illustrated by Tom Heard

Published by MAVERICK ARTS PUBLISHING LTD
Studio 11, City Business Centre, 6 Brighton Road,
Horsham, West Sussex, RH13 5BB
© Maverick Arts Publishing Limited May 2023
+44 (0)1403 256941

A CIP catalogue record for this book is available at the British Library.

ISBN 978-1-84886-962-2

www.maverickbooks.co.uk

This book is rated as: Gold Band (Guided Reading)

The Fairly Scary Fairy

By Kate Poels

Illustrated by Tom Heard

Chapter 1

Kip the fairy was cross.

Tomorrow was Name Day at school, and she still hadn't earned her very own fairy name.

Miss Wing, her teacher, had given out all the temporary name badges in class.

Pod was now called the Good Fairy. Mags was the Wise Fairy, Gert was the

Funny Fairy and even Trix had been given a badge that named her as the Cheeky Fairy.

But there had been no badge for Kip and time was running out.

"You have to earn a fairy name," said Kip's friend, Blink. "Think of something you are really good at."

"The trouble is," Kip said, "every time I think of a cool new name that could be mine, I can't earn it."

"What have you tried?" Blink asked her.

"Water Fairy," said Kip. "But I can't swim."

"Yes, I can see how that would be a problem," said Blink.

"I've tried Love Fairy, but everyone got cross with me when I tried to make them fall in love. I even tried Sad Fairy but my friends kept finding ways of cheering me up."

Kip and Blink sat side by side on spotted toadstools in the school field.

By the time the bell rang to tell all the fairies it was time to go home, they still hadn't thought of a good name for Kip.

Chapter 2

Kip stomped up the road in a very bad mood. She didn't see the huge muddy puddle until it was too late. Her legs went up and her bottom went down with a SPLAT! Kip was covered in sticky mud and this made her crosser than ever.

"Oh dear," said a passing elf.

"Grrrr," growled Kip. She was so cross that the growl came out loud and strong.

The poor elf was very scared and ran away quickly.

Kip stood up and tried to wipe the mud from her face, but she just made it worse.
She looked down at her best skirt. It was ruined, and so was her soft green jumper.

"Hrrrumph," she said so loudly that a squirrel ran up the closest tree in fright.

Honk and Plonk, the twins who lived at the end of Kip's road, burst into tears when she stomped past and they rushed inside their house.

"Goodness!" said Kip to herself. "I didn't know I could be so scary."

Chapter 3

As soon as she got home, Kip had a shower and put on clean clothes. She was thinking about how she had scared the elf, the squirrel and Honk and Plonk.

'Maybe that's the fairy I'm supposed to be,' she thought. 'Perhaps my name could be the Scary Fairy.'

She didn't love the idea but there wasn't

much time left until Name Day and this was the best she had.

On the way to school the next day, Kip saw Honk and Plonk in their garden.

"BOO!" she shouted.

Instead of screaming, the twins just giggled and waved at Kip.

Kip thought this was odd, but she carried on her way until she came across a group of young fairies playing with acorns.

Kip put on her scariest face and jumped into the middle of their game.

"Gahhhhh!" she yelled.
Some of the fairies looked cross and some looked shocked but nobody looked scared.
"Aren't I scary?" Kip asked.

"No," said one of the fairies. "But you did ruin our game."

Kip looked sad as the group picked up their acorns and walked away.

"I thought you were fairly scary," said a very small fairy with red hair.

"I don't want to be Kip the Fairly Scary Fairy," she said crossly to herself.

Chapter 4

Kip sat under a tree and kicked at a pebble with her toe.

"I can make you scary," said a voice from the tree.

Kip looked around and saw a face in the bark of the tree.

"Who are you?" Kip asked.

"I am the Wishing Tree," said the voice. "If scary is what you want then I can make it happen."

Kip thought about it. Perhaps this was the plan she had been waiting for. It might be the only chance she had.

"Yes please," said Kip.

She closed her eyes and felt an odd fizzing in her skin. When she opened her eyes, the face in the tree had vanished.

Kip looked around but the only person she could see was a mouse. The mouse saw Kip too. He squeaked in alarm and ran off.

"Wow!" said Kip. "Maybe I am scary again."

She carried on her way to school and saw that everyone who walked past her was really scared.

"I must get my new name now!" she said.

Chapter 5

The playground was full when Kip went in but soon, everyone vanished inside.

Kip wasn't sure she liked being quite so scary, but she kept thinking about her new fairy name.

She walked through the school to find Miss Wing, but Miss Wing yelled and shut herself in the cupboard when she saw Kip.

This was no good at all!

Nobody would come near Kip, and that made her very upset. Suddenly, she didn't care about a new name, she just wanted to be Kip who the other fairies liked to talk to.

Sadly, she walked away from school and found a quiet place in the park to sit on her own where she couldn't scare anyone.

Kip sniffed back a tear and was about to go home when she saw a big grey cat marching down the street. The cat looked mean and hungry, so Kip hid behind a tree and watched him stalk past.

"That was close!" she said to herself. But then she noticed where the cat was heading. Straight towards the school where the naming ceremony was about to begin!

He was licking his lips and waving his tail and Kip didn't know what to do. All Kip's friends would be out on the school field, and it would be easy for the cat to get them.

Someone needed to stop the cat, but Kip was just one small fairy and no match for a mean, hungry cat. Then Kip remembered something. She might be small, but she was also really scary.

There was no choice for Kip if she wanted to save her friends, so she put on her bravest face and ran after the cat.

Chapter 6

The cat got to the school field just as Miss Wing handed out a final name badge to Pod the Good Fairy.

The cat looked at all the fairies and licked his lips. He got ready to pounce…

...but Kip was fast! She ran up to the cat and tugged on his tail.

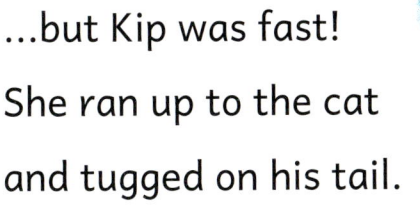

The cat hissed in anger and turned around, showing his claws. But when he saw Kip, his anger turned to fear. He yowled and howled and all of his fur stood up on end.

Then, he ran away from the scary fairy as fast as he could.

Kip felt a fizz in her body, and then she heard a big clap and a cheer. She saw that all the fairies were smiling at her.

The Wishing Tree's magic must have just worn off.

Miss Wing came over to Kip.

"Thank you, Kip," she said. "You saved us all. Now come and collect your new fairy name badge."

Kip felt so proud as Miss Wing pinned the perfect badge to her jumper and everyone cheered.

Kip had found her true fairy name.

She was the Brave Fairy.

The End

Book Bands for Guided Reading

The Institute of Education book banding system is a scale of colours that reflects the various levels of reading difficulty. The bands are assigned by taking into account the content, the language style, the layout and phonics. Word, phrase and sentence level work is also taken into consideration.

Maverick Early Readers are a bright, attractive range of books covering the pink to white bands. All of these books have been book banded for guided reading to the industry standard and edited by a leading educational consultant.

To view the whole Maverick Readers scheme, visit our website at www.maverickearlyreaders.com

Or scan the QR code above to view our scheme instantly!